THE
SEVEN
WONDERS
OF
THE
WORLD

◆

Kenneth McLeish

illustrated by Sharon Pallent

CAMBRIDGE
UNIVERSITY PRESS

CONTENTS

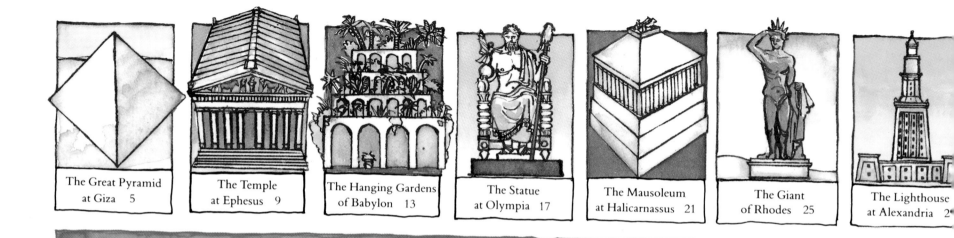

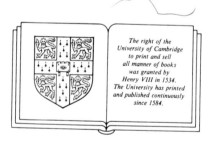

The right of the University of Cambridge to print and sell all manner of books was granted by Henry VIII in 1534. The University has printed and published continuously since 1584.

Published by the Press Syndicate of the University of Cambridge
The Pitt Building, Trumpington Street, Cambridge CB2 1RP
40 West 20th Street, New York, NY 10011-4211, USA
10 Stamford Road, Oakleigh, Melbourne 3166, Australia

© Cambridge University Press 1985

First published 1985; fourth printing 1994
First paperback edition 1989; fifth printing 1994

Printed in Hong Kong by Wing King Tong Co., Ltd.

Library of Congress catalogue card number: 84–21389

British Library cataloguing in publication data

McLeish, Kenneth
The Seven Wonders of the World.

1. Seven Wonders of the World - Juvenile literature
I. Title
930'.0982'2   N5333

ISBN 0 521 26538 X hardback
ISBN 0 521 37911 3 paperback

DS

THE SEVEN WONDERS

Travel nowadays is easy. Railways and roads criss-cross the countryside, and there are bicycles, cars and buses everywhere. Trains and planes carry millions of people abroad each year, and there are guidebooks to tell us where to go and what to see.

Three thousand years ago, none of these things existed. There were no mechanical vehicles; apart from sailing-ships (which used the wind), all vehicles used animal or human muscle-power. Roads were few and far between. They were dusty in summer and muddy in winter, and led from one town or village to the next with no overall, countrywide plan. Travellers, by road or sea, were easy prey for highwaymen and pirates. If you set out on a journey of more than 50 kilometres (30 miles), there was less than a 50–50 chance that you would arrive the same day, all in one piece and unattacked.

Because travelling was so

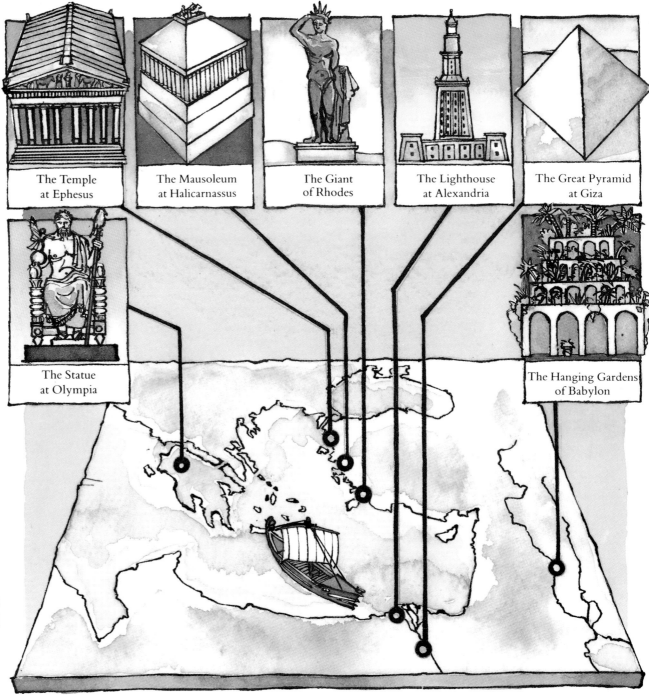

The Temple at Ephesus

The Mausoleum at Halicarnassus

The Giant of Rhodes

The Lighthouse at Alexandria

The Great Pyramid at Giza

The Statue at Olympia

The Hanging Gardens of Babylon

chancy, most people stayed at home. Merchants, traders and soldiers were the main travellers, and they went in large numbers and with armed guards. Ordinary people seldom ventured beyond their own villages or towns, and all they knew of the wonders of 'foreign parts' was from travellers' tales, stories as likely to be made-up as fact. (Who knew, for example, if Polyphemus, the one-eyed giant who ate Odysseus' crew in Homer's story *The Odyssey*, was fact or fiction? Very few people would have visited his part of the world to see.)

By the time of Alexander the Great (356–323 BC), everything had changed. Alexander was a conqueror: his ambition was to make the world one single empire. He began with Greece, and then moved into Persia (a gigantic kingdom, as large as the present-day USA). His soldiers travelled the length and breadth of Persia, conquering as they went, and only stopped when they reached the river Beas (in what is now India). From being prince of a small mountain kingdom in northern Greece, Alexander came to rule an empire a hundred times as big.

As travel became more secure, people moved about more. There were Greek towns everywhere, with a friendly welcome for visitors; soldiers kept the roads and sea-crossings reasonably clear of robbers. People became curious about the other parts of Alexander's enormous empire, eager to go and see for themselves what they had once only heard about in tales. It was the beginning of tourism.

Guidebooks with wonder-lists were written as long ago as the sixth century BC, but some time in the third century BC (no one knows exactly when), a list appeared of *the* Seven Wonders of the World. It was a good idea – but why just seven? In the huge Greek empire there were far more than seven wonders, and just as much of the world lay outside the empire as inside it, with plentiful wonders of its own. But the idea of seven wonders, seven spectacular sights to visit, quickly became popular, and the list of seven wonders has fascinated people ever since.

The seven wonders were skilfully chosen to encourage travellers. Apart from the Hanging Gardens of Babylon in the east and the Statue of Zeus in the west, they all lay in the centre of the Greek empire, in places beside seas or navigable rivers, and they were equally easy to reach from east or west. None are natural wonders (as, say, the Grand Canyon or Niagara Falls are natural); all were made by human effort, and show human technology at its most stunning and inventive. They were like an advertisement for the skills of the people in the enlarged Greek empire, a proof to everyone of how civilised and organised they were.

Author's note:
Only one of the Seven Wonders of the World (the Great Pyramid) still exists, and exact measurements for the others are hard to find. The measurements in this book are based on surviving fragments, or on the most likely-seeming ancient reports and eye-witness descriptions. But they give an impression only – rather as we might today, if we were asked to give an account in words of Stonehenge, Niagara Falls or the Sydney Harbour Bridge.

THE GREAT PYRAMID

The ancient Egyptians believed that a human being has two separate existences, one as body and one as spirit. We all know what the body-world is like, because we live in it; the Egyptians thought that the spirit-world was just the same, and that the spirit needed furniture, food, clothes, money, even games and toys, just as the body does. They thought that after people's bodies died, their spirits went on living, swooping freely about the spirit-world during the night but coming back to their bodies each morning for food and rest.

Because they believed that the body was the spirit's house, the ancient Egyptians wanted to preserve their bodies for as long as possible after death. Their funeral priests began by removing all the soft parts (brain, lungs, heart, liver, intestines) and pickling them in gigantic clay jars. Then they packed the rest of the body with preserving salts and wrapped it tightly in bandages (so making what we nowadays call a 'mummy'). Lastly, they laid the mummy to rest in a tomb, with all the clothes, food, money and other things the person might need in his or her spirit-life.

Poor people's tombs were ordinary graves, holes in the ground or hillside caves. Better-off people's tombs were larger, stone buildings anything from table-size to the size of a garden shed or smallish house. The most important people of all, kings, queens and priests, had pyramids: vast piles of chiselled stone blocks, houses for the spirit as spacious as the body's palaces in earthly life.

The Great Pyramid was built as a spirit-palace for King Kufu about 2590–2570 BC. (When the Greeks listed the Seven Wonders of the World 2300 years later, they turned his name into its Greek form Cheops, and the pyramid is sometimes known as Cheops' Pyramid.) It is the main building in a town of the dead near Giza (a suburb of modern Cairo beside the river Nile). Around it are the remains of more than eighty other

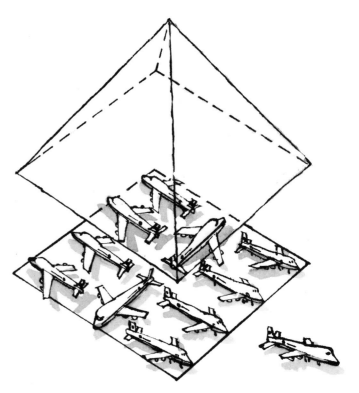

pyramids, as well as temples, tombs, altars and ceremonial roadways. Beside the pyramids, as if guarding them, crouches the Sphinx, a stone lion with a bearded, human face. The whole place, pyramids, roads, temples, Sphinx, is constantly scoured by desert sand, which has pitted and scarred the surface of the stone.

The Great Pyramid is enormous, a hand-made hill. Its base-area would allow parking-space for ten modern jumbo-jets, and it is as high as three space-shuttles (plus launch-vehicles) stacked on top of one another nose to tail. From its vast base it tapers to a point 10 cm (4 inches) wide which was originally gold-plated and glittered in the sun. The pyramid was built from more than two million stone blocks, each of them twice the weight of a modern car. If the pyramid was hollow (instead of solid, except for the burial-chamber right in the centre and the passages leading to it), it would comfortably hold the Houses of Parliament and St Paul's Cathedral from London, or the Pentagon and the Capitol from Washington, D.C. If the stones were broken up and made into a wall 30 cm (1 foot) wide and 1 metre (3 feet) high, it would stretch all the way round France.

Even today, with dynamite to blast the rocks, and cranes and bulldozers to shift them, it would take years of effort to build such an enormous pile. The Egyptians made do with muscle-power and brains. To quarry the rocks (from cliff-sites sometimes many kilometres upriver), they chiselled holes in the sandstone cliffs, then hammered wooden wedges into them and soaked the wedges with water. The wedges swelled and the rocks split. When each 2- to 3-ton block was ready, they raised it with levers on to a huge wooden sledge, and harnessed a team of men to it.

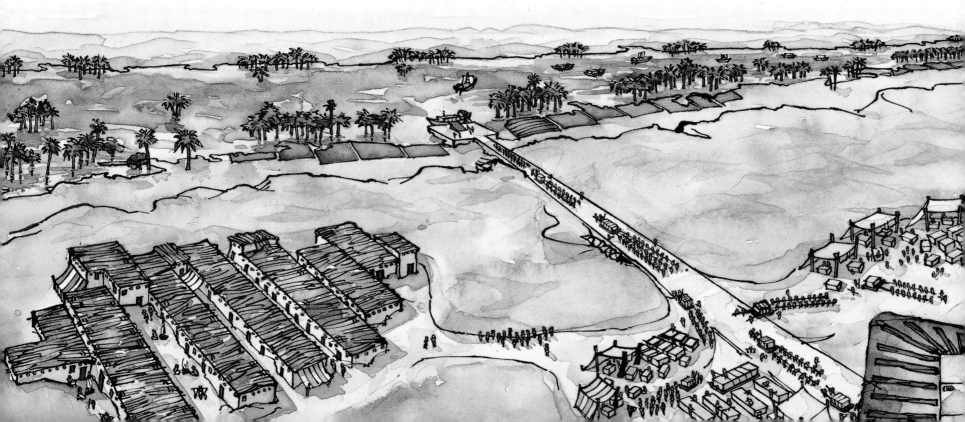

Perhaps a hundred men pulled, while ten more lubricated the sledge-runners (with water, animal-fat or milk). Like ants dragging along a burden a hundred times their own size, they hauled the stone to the river Nile, floated it on rafts down-river to the building-site at Giza, heaved and tugged it up sloping earth ramps and fitted it in place. Modern archaeologists have calculated that if one gang of men could move ten stones a month, it would have taken 70,000 to 80,000 men about five years to build the pyramid.

When the basic pyramid was finished, the builders faced it with smooth stones to make its sides sheer and flat. (These stones were later removed for other building-work, and the sides of the pyramid are now like gigantic flights of steps.) Inside, passageways led to a burial-chamber about the size of a small modern house (10 × 5 metres, or 34 × 17 feet; 6 metres, or 19 feet, high). Its walls were of polished pink granite and inside was a sarcophagus (coffin-box) carved so perfectly from a single stone that if you hit it it made a sound like a bell.

At the king's funeral, his body was brought downriver on the royal barge, carried in procession to the pyramid, down the passageway and into the chamber, where it was laid to rest with all the belongings his spirit would need in the afterlife, and even the mummified bodies of his favourite pets. The chamber doorway was plugged with stone, and a curse was placed on anyone who broke it down. Then the priests and mourners went away, and the builders filled up the passageway with rubble, hid the entrance, and moved on to their next enormous job leaving Kufu's body and spirit to enjoy the afterlife in peace.

THE GREAT PYRAMID
Date: c. 2590–2570 BC
Height: c. 147 metres (481 feet)
Base: 230 × 230 metres (756 × 756 feet)
Base area: 5.3 hectares (13 acres)
Weight: c. 5.4 million tons

THE TEMPLE AT EPHESUS

Over 3300 years ago, a boulder plummeted out of the sky and killed the king of Apashash, a town near the mouth of the river Cayster (in what is now western Turkey). The boulder was roughly human-shape, and was as knobbly as a pine-cone, covered in bumps, lumps, hummocks and stubs like some monstrous living thing. The superstitious river-people (who did not know that the boulder was a meteorite) thought that it was the goddess Mother Earth, creator of all living things, and that she had killed the king to punish his wickedness. The lumps and bumps, they thought, were the goddess' children, or breasts where her babies could suck her milk. They put the stone in a grove of sacred trees, and worshipped it.

As time passed and more and more people settled near the river-mouth, Apashash prospered. Its harbour was ideal for fishing and for trade (for example with the nearby Greek island of Samos). Its

fields, covered every spring with silt from the flooded river, were lush and fertile. Above all, visitors flocked there to worship the goddess. Greek visitors changed the town's name from Apashash to Ephesus, and identified the goddess not as Mother Earth but as Artemis, one of their own goddesses of fertility and birth.

In the sixth century BC King Croesus of Lydia, one of the richest and most god-fearing people in the world, visited Ephesus to worship the goddess. He decided to replace her mud-hut shrine with a gigantic new temple, a tribute not only to

her greatness but to his own magnificence and generosity.

Croesus hired a team of Greek architects to build the temple. They had recently designed a temple for the island of Samos, and had experience with huge buildings and difficult, marshy sites. Experience with marshland was crucial, as the only part of the Cayster plain free from earthquakes, and therefore suitable for large stone buildings, was waterlogged.

The builders chose a site 1 hectare (2½ acres) in area, and cleared it of trees and undergrowth. They used the wood to make charcoal, and wherever marshy pools appeared, filled them in with alternate layers of charcoal and sheepskins. In summer, when the area dried out, they covered it with rubble and hard-packed earth. These were the temple's foundations.

While this work went on, other workmen quarried marble in the nearby hills. There were two kinds of blocks, rectangular and cylindrical: each was as tall as a human being and wide as a cart.

The workmen levered the rectangular blocks on to wheels and axles, harnessed oxen to them and dragged them the 13 kilometres (8 miles) to the temple-site. As for the cylinders, they simply fitted cart-frames over them, as if they were wheels, and trundled them away.

If four people stand close together, shoulder to shoulder in a square, they take up about 1 square metre (just over 1 square yard) of ground. On the site cleared for the temple, 45,000 people could have stood this way: the population of a sizeable town. The builders paved the area with marble blocks, and built the temple on top of them.

As you climbed the steps to the temple doors, the most impressive part of the building would have been the columns which supported the roof. There were 127 of them, in rows all round the building. Each column was made from six or seven of the huge cylindrical blocks from the marble-quarry, and they stood 6 metres (20 feet) apart. The columns supported another enormous rectangle of marble blocks (the same size as the temple-base), and above it a sloping roof. Every part of the temple that you could see was covered with carvings and paintings of myth-stories, brightly coloured and decorated with gold leaf. Inside the temple, almost hidden among the

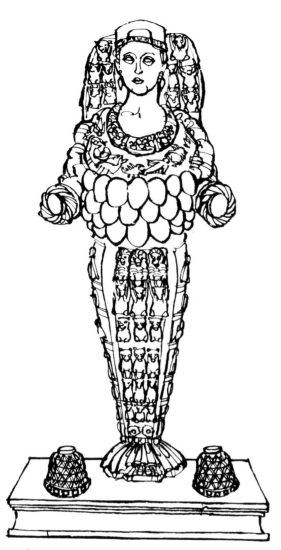

columns, was the home of the goddess – and though the old meteorite figure was now reshaped and recarved, the goddess's skirt still teemed with animals and her front hung with breasts, exactly as before.

Croesus' temple, and the magnificent park around it, made Ephesus a place of pilgrimage for two hundred years. Then, in 356 BC, a lunatic called Herostratos set fire to it. No one knows why he did it ('to make myself famous', he claimed afterwards). All history tells us is that he set fire to it on the same day as Alexander the Great was born, and that when Alexander grew up and visited Ephesus, he was so impressed by the ruins that he paid to have the temple rebuilt, even larger and more spectacular than in Croesus' time.

The new temple remained a wonder of the world for five hundred years. It brought prosperity to the whole area, to traders, innkeepers, guides, priests, prophets, and above all makers and sellers of souvenirs. (Favourite souvenirs were models of the temple, or of the goddess's statue, in gold, silver or clay depending on the price. When St Paul preached in Ephesus in AD 52, and converted hundreds of visitors to Christianity, the silversmiths started a riot against him for ruining their business.)

The destruction of the temple came in the third century AD. First it was plundered by Goths, sweeping south from the Black Sea to plunder the Roman empire; then its stones were used to build a Christian church nearby; then the river changed course and swamped the remains with silt. In 1870 an Englishman called Wood excavated the site and found many fragments of sculpture and architecture from both temples. He brought them back to the British Museum where they are on display today. Nothing is left at Ephesus except a few blocks from the foundations and a single rebuilt column – and in the museum, a statue of the mysterious earth-goddess whose shrine it was.

THE TEMPLE AT EPHESUS

Note: the temple is sometimes known today as Diana's temple: Diana is the roman name for the goddess Artemis. The measurements are of Croesus' temple as it was rebuilt for Alexander.

Dates: Croesus' temple *c.* 560 BC; Alexander's rebuilding *c.* 330 BC onwards
Base: 73 metres (239 feet) × 133 metres (436 feet)
Base area: 1 hectare (2.4 acres)
Total height: c. 34 metres (*c.* 110 feet)

THE HANGING GARDENS

The country now called Iraq is like a scoop of fertile land surrounded on three sides by deserts or mountains and on the fourth by the Persian Gulf. Two rivers run through it, the Tigris and the Euphrates, and their flooding and subsiding (like the river Nile's in Egypt) make the wedge of land between them some of the richest farmland on Earth. Right at its heart, on the banks of the river Euphrates, the ancient city of Babylon once stood.

Babylon, the capital of Babylonia, was at its peak from about 620 to 550 BC. It was ruled by warrior-kings, and the Babylonian empire included all the towns and peoples round about. Barges and merchant-ships on the river, and mule-trains and camel-trains overland, brought traders from all parts of the world, eager to barter the wealth of their own countries for Babylonian corn. The city's treasuries bulged with gold, silver, ebony, ivory, silk and

precious stones; its streets, fields and warehouses bustled with slaves; its walls and temples glittered with ornament, and its parks were filled with plants and trees from every corner of the world.

In 605 BC Nebuchadnezzar became king of Babylon. He was the most successful warrior-king in all its history, and defeated its enemies on every side: Egyptians, Elamites, Syrians and Carians. His soldiers travelled as far west as the Dead Sea, sacked Jerusalem and

took its entire population back to Babylon as prisoners-of-war. The only people Nebuchadnezzar did not try to conquer were the Medes, who lived in wild mountain country far to Babylon's north. Istead of fighting, Nebuchadnezzar won the Medes over in another way: he married their princess Amytis, and made a friendly alliance between the two nations.

This is where the story of the Hanging Gardens begins. Amytis had never lived anywhere but hill-country, and was used to mountains, but Babylonia was flat (like modern East Anglia, the mid-western United States, or the central plains of Australia). There was not a hill in sight. The story goes that as Amytis watched Nebuchadnezzar's workmen building walls, temples, city gates and a magnificent new royal palace, she pined for her native hills – and Nebuchadnezzar ordered the building of the Hanging Gardens to remind her of home.

The words 'Hanging Gardens' suggest ledges or terraces like gigantic modern window-boxes, filled with overhanging plants. In fact the real Gardens 'hung' only in the sense that they were built not at ground level but high overhead, on arches, overlooking the city walls and the river Euphrates. Some vegetation certainly did overhang, but the gardens chiefly contained trees, shrubs, flowers and other upward-growing plants. From the palace, the effect must have been like looking out on a jungly mountainside (exactly what Nebuchadnezzar hoped his homesick princess would enjoy). From ground level it must have looked as if a whole park had risen up and was floating, or hanging, in mid-air.

The first stage of building the gardens was to make a series of brick archways like those supporting a present-day bridge or viaduct. They were ten storeys high, the height of the city walls, and had a shaded courtyard underneath. On top of them the workmen built brick terraces, in long straight rows like a giant's staircase. They lined the terraces with lead (to keep the water in), and covered them with thick layers of earth from the fields below. This gave them half a dozen enormous flowerbeds (each larger than a modern tennis-court), and in them

they planted every imaginable kind of tree and plant, importing them from all over the kingdom by ox-cart and river-barge. The planning was so exact, and slave-labour was so plentiful, that the gardens could have been layered and stocked in a few days rather than in weeks or months. It is easy to imagine Amytis' delight and surprise when she saw, one morning, a whole park, shady with palm trees, bright with flowers and buzzing with birds and insects, hovering in the air where there had been nothing but brick terraces a week or so before.

Babylonia was a country of plant-growers, farmers, and gardeners. They saw to it that the Hanging Gardens were not just a wonder for a few weeks or months, but would last for season after season without withering. To keep them green and growing in that hot, dry climate, the main need was for running water, and they devised an irrigation system which sent streams and rivulets endlessly tumbling down the terraces. They dug an underground cistern, lined it

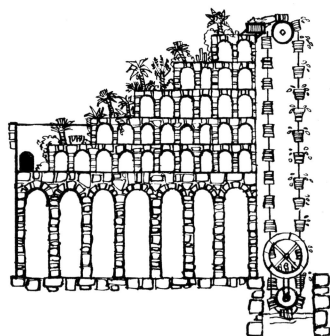

with stone and supplied it with a constant supply of water from the river. Beside it they built a chimney-shaped tower as high as the topmost terrace of the Gardens. At the tower's top hung a huge wheel, and round it passed an endless chain of water-buckets. Slaves down below worked a treadmill, day in day out, and the buckets travelled up the chimney, emptied their water into the terrace, and passed down again to the cistern for another load.

The Hanging Gardens lasted far beyond Nebuchadnezzar's and Amytis' time. In fact no one knows exactly when they disappeared. Babylon's power ended in 539 BC (when it was captured by Cyrus, the founder of the Persian empire). But the Hanging Gardens lived on: they still existed in the time of Alexander the Great, two hundred years later, and continued for generations afterwards, visited by thousands of people as one of the Seven Wonders of the World. Sadly, nowadays, when the whole city of Babylon is no more than a pile of dusty rubble, no trace at all is left of them.

THE HANGING GARDENS
Date: c. 600 BC
Supporting archways: 24 metres (80 feet) high
Total area of gardens: 31 × 31 metres (100 × 100 feet)
Height of gardens: the lowest terrace was the level of the top of the archways, i.e. 24 metres (80 feet) above ground. Each succeeding terrace was about 3 metres (10 feet) higher, until the topmost terrace was about 40 metres (130 feet) above ground-level.
Area of each terrace: 30 metres (100 feet) × 5 metres (16 feet) (that is, if there were half a dozen terraces; no one knows for sure)

THE STATUE AT OLYMPIA

Every four years, at the beginning of summer, tens of thousands of people made their way to the flat plain of Olympia, beside the Greek river Alpheios. The river was deep, and never dried up in summer (as many Greek rivers do); the valley beside it was rich farmland, famous for its almond-trees and for the cattle which browsed in the water-meadows.

It was not farming, however, which drew most visitors, but a three-month-long religious festival ending in the Olympic Games. Every Greek town and city sent worshippers to the festival and competitors to the Games, and there were crowds of spectators and supporters, just as at large sporting occasions nowadays. The Games (racing, boxing, wrestling, long jump and archery) took place in the last five days of the festival, and the weeks beforehand were spent in prayers, sacrifices, processions, training and sightseeing. The first festival was held in 776 BC, and the

Games happened so regularly after that, every four years, that the Greeks used them as a kind of calendar (saying such things as 'He was born in the year when So-and-so won the wrestling at the forty-fifth Olympic Games').

Olympia was not the only place where Games were held: there were over three hundred other festivals, at places all over Greece. But the Olympic Games were the biggest of all, and were sacred to the most important of all the Greek gods, Olympian Zeus. All the

events were in his honour; the processions and sacrifices were made to him; his altar stood in the centre of the site, and a hundred cattle were sacrificed on it as the main part of each festival; his temple stood in its own grounds behind the altar, looking across at the stadium and crowds beyond.

The original temple was small and simple, and housed small statues of Zeus and his queen Hera. But in the fifth century BC the citizens of the nearby town of Elis decided to build Zeus a new

17

temple, better suited to his rank as king of the gods, and a new statue to place inside it.

The temple was magnificent. It measured 64 × 27 metres (210 feet × 89 feet), and was built of stone blocks as big as boats. It was surrounded by thirty-four massive columns which supported a roof whose triangular fronts were decorated with splendid statues. Every part of the walls and columns was covered with stucco (kind of plaster made with marble dust) and details were painted on top. The deeds of Herakles were carved on plaques above the entrances, and the roof was made o solid marble tiles.

If the temple was beautiful, the statue of Zeus was even more spectacular. It showed him sitting in majesty on his royal throne, and towered to fill the whole sanctuary, nearly seven times mortal height. Its face was so high up (only 30 cm, 1 foot, below the temple roof) that viewing-platforms were built along the temple walls inside, so that people could climb up and see the god's expression close at hand. Only two statues like it had ever been built before in Greece, statues of Athene made for the Acropolis in Athens, and the Olympian priests used the same team of artists, led by the sculptor Phidias.

Phidias and his workmen first put up a hefty wooden pillar, as tall as a ship's mast and set into a limestone base: this was the statue's main support. All round it they fastened a wooden framework, carefully pegged together in the form of the god sitting on his throne. When this skeleton was complete, they covered it with sheets of ivory (for flesh) and moulded gold (for clothing) and camouflaged the joins. Zeus' feet rested on a stool decorated with gold lions and carvings of scenes from myth. A carved olive-crown was on his head, his right hand supported a small, ivory-and-gold statue of Victory and his left hand held his royal sceptre with a golden eagle perched on top. His robe and sandals were gold, and every part of his clothes was inlaid with animals and *fleurs-de-lis*. His throne, his footstool and the screens round the statue's limestone base were covered with paintings and carvings, and were a mass of ebony, ivory and precious stones.

Despite the statue's fabulous richness, no one ever tried to steal

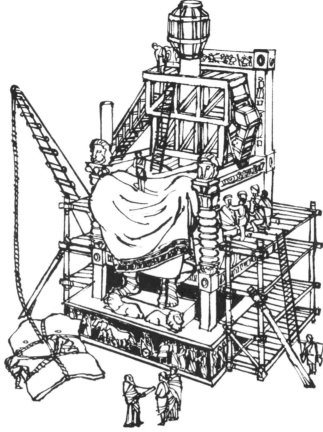

from it – people were too afraid of the god's vengeance to risk attacking him. It stood as one of the world's most glittering wonders for 800 years. Then, in AD 391, the Roman emperor Theodosius passed a law banning all religions except Christianity and closing down all non-Christian shrines. Zeus-worship came to an end, and the Olympic Games ended with it (it

was 1500 years before they began again). Workmen took the statue t bits, shipped it to Constantinople (Theodosius' capital city on the shores of the Bosporus: modern Istanbul), and rebuilt it in the grounds of a palace there. Some years afterwards, it was struck by lightning and totally destroyed – and two centuries after that the river Alpheios flooded Olympia and engulfed plain, altar, stadium, temple and all the other remains in 3 metres (10 feet) of mud. It was almost as if Zeus, god of rain and lightning, had done exactly as his worshippers thought he would, an taken revenge for the plundering of his holiest earthly shrine.

Just over a hundred years ago, archaeologists began excavating the site. Now the mud has gone and you can walk round the remains of the temples and see the plinth in the temple of Zeus where his statue used to sit.

THE STATUE OF ZEUS
Date: c. 438–430 BC
Limestone base: 6.55 metres × 9.93 metres (2½ feet × 32½ feet); 1 metre (3 feet) high
Height of statue: 13 metres (43 feet)

THE MAUSOLEUM

From 377 to 353 BC Mausolus was the ruler of Caria (the south-western corner of what is now Turkey). Caria was part of the huge Persian empire, and Mausolus acted as Governor for the Persian king and was supposed to be a loyal servant to him. But the king lived a month's march away, and his soldiers never visited Mausolus' rocky province. Mausolus ruled as he pleased.

He decided to build a new capital, a fortified city as hard to capture as it was magnificent to look at. He chose the little town of Halicarnassus (modern Bodrum), on the coast of the Aegean Sea opposite the Greek island of Cos. It lay in a cup-shaped hollow protected on three sides by hills and on the fourth by the sea. The bay was wide and deep, and was sheltered by two arms of land shaped like a crab's pincers. If Mausolus' ships blocked the narrow channel in between, they could keep all enemy warships out.

Mausolus set about making Halicarnassus a fit capital-city for a warrior-prince. His workmen deepened the harbour and used the dredged-up sand to strengthen its protecting arms. On land, they laid out paved squares, streets and houses for the ordinary citizens, and on one side of the harbour, where the castle now stands, they built a massive fortress-palace for Mausolus, positioned so that there were clear views out to sea and inland to the hills, the two directions from which enemies might attack. Lastly, they built walls and watchtowers on the landward side, and put up a Greek-style theatre and a temple to Ares, the Greek god of war.

Safe in their castle-town, Mausolus and his queen Artemisia prospered. Taxes from the whole of Caria poured into Halicarnassus, and Mausolus and Artemisia spent them in beautifying the town, adding statues, temples and buildings of gleaming marble, designed and carved by the finest Greek craftsmen money could buy.

In the centre of the town, midway between the harbour and the hills, Mausolus planned to put the most impressive building of all: a resting-place for his body after death, a tomb that would forever show the world how rich and powerful he and his queen had been. Mausolus hired architects, set gangs of workmen to clear the site, and ordered shiploads of marble from the island of Paros and from many other quarries over the whole Greek world.

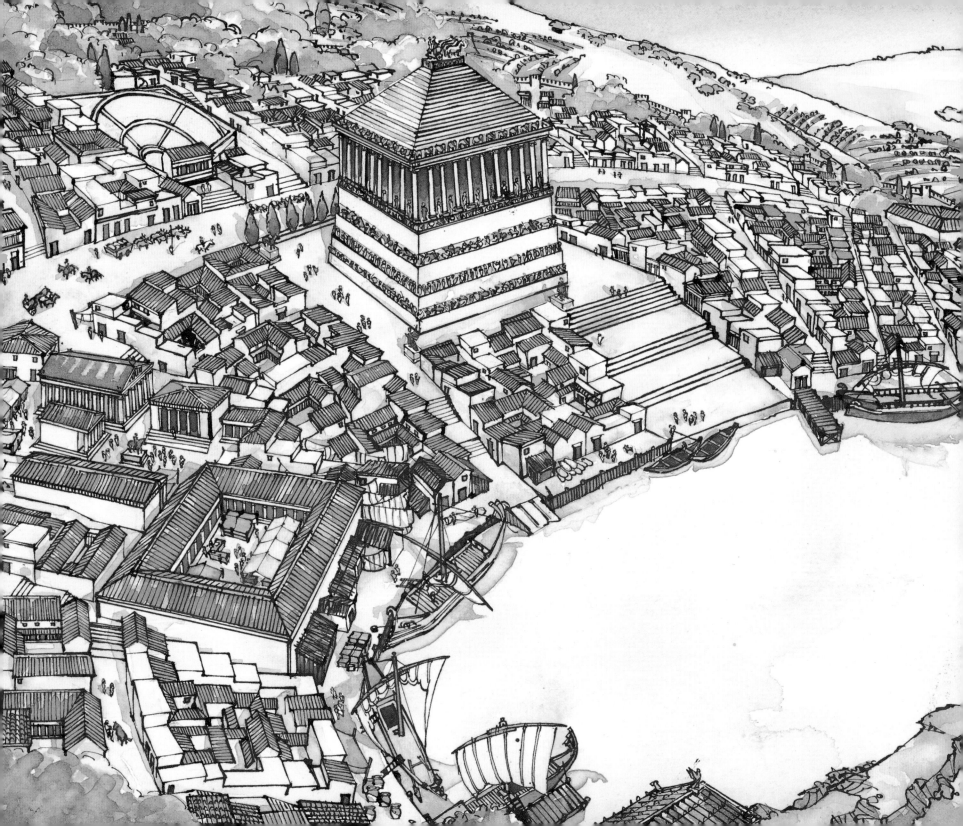

Mausolus) were used to designing temples, buildings meant not for human beings but for gods. They built for Mausolus and Artemisia on the same superhuman scale. The work began with an underground tomb-chamber, carved from solid rock, in which the ashes of the royal couple would forever lie in their golden caskets. (Its doorway, and the marble staircase leading down to it, were blocked with rubble after the royal funerals, to keep out looters.) Above it was a massive rectangular stone base (the size of a modern ice-skating rink and six storeys high); on top of that was a building the size and shape of a Greek temple, surrounded by thirty-six columns and thirty-six statues. The building's roof was like a stone pyramid with twenty-four steps, and on its flat top was a statue-group of a chariot pulled by four horses. The styles of the three parts of the building were Carian (the base), Greek (the temple) and Egyptian (the pyramid), and so symbolised the three civilisations Mausolus hoped to bring together in his new city.

Mausolus died before the tomb was finished, but Queen Artemisia urged the architects to continue. (In fact, the story goes that she spent so much that the state went bankrupt, but that the architects and their men were so excited by the work they were doing that they finished it without wages.)

The architects who planned the Mausoleum (as it was called, after

23

Because of its size, the Mausoleum must have been visible far out to sea, and the architects made it even more striking by the gleaming finish they laid over every part of it. They covered its flat surfaces with marble blocks, and decorated it on all four sides at different levels with carved battle-scenes, and with dozens of statues arranged in groups. Some groups showed the king hunting or receiving offerings, others showed the gods and heroes of Greek mythology. The workmen rubbed the relief-sculptures and statues

smooth with sand, painted them in bright colours and polished them till they shone.

Unlike a temple, which had rooms inside, the Mausoleum was probably solid all the way through. As a building, it was useless: its purpose was to impress visitors with the power and wealth of the monarch whose tomb it was. Shortly after it was finished Queen Artemisia died and was buried beside her husband – and shortly after *that*, Alexander the Great conquered Halicarnassus and added Caria to his empire. Halicarnassus became an unimportant provincial town once again, a backwater visited mainly by tourists.

Mausolus and Artemisia lay undisturbed in their underground vault for 1800 years. Then, in the thirteenth century AD, an earthquake threw down the columns and roof of the Mausoleum, and in 1489 the Christians, who had made Halicarnassus a stronghold against the Turks, began using the stones of the base to build new castle walls and breaking up the sculptures to

use as mortar. By 1522, when they had demolished most of the building, they discovered the tomb chamber. The story goes that they found much gold there, but it was stolen by pirates, and only a few gold ornaments survive today. In 1857 British archaeologists began excavating the remains. They found no trace of the actual building except the foundations of the base, but rescued some of the huge statues and carved battle-scenes and carted them to the British Museum in London, where they can still be seen today. The word 'Mausoleum' lives on, too. It has come to mean a stately and magnificent tomb put up in memory of some important person and there are mausoleums to kings, queens, generals, presidents and emperors in many countries of the world.

THE MAUSOLEUM
Date: c. 365–350 BC
Height: c. 43 metres (140 feet)
Base: 39 metres (127 feet) × 33 metres (108 feet)
Base area: 1274 square metres (13,716 square feet or ⅓ acre)

THE GIANT OF RHODES

The people of Rhodes thought that Helios the sun-god favoured their island more than any other place on earth. All over the island, they set up statues in his honour, some a few centimetres or inches high, others as big as houses. The finest of all were in the town of Rhodes itself, the beautiful capital city the islanders built for themselves in 408 BC. It had wide streets, fine public buildings and spacious houses; it was protected by a stone wall and towering gates, and it had two sheltered harbours separated by a long tongue of land.

Rhodes was a trading island, and its riches came from welcoming every merchant or visitor who cared to call. The islanders liked to keep neutral, to take no part in other people's wars. But about 323 BC, when Alexander the Great died and his generals began squabbling over his empire, they broke their rule and sided with Ptolemy, the general who controlled Egypt. At once Ptolemy's rival Antigonus, who controlled Greece, ordered the Rhodians to favour him instead, and when they refused he sent his son Demetrius (nicknamed 'The City-sacker') to destroy their town.

Demetrius' nickname was well-earned; he had captured every single city he attacked. He invaded Rhodes with 200 warships, an army of fighting men and no fewer than 30,000 engineers. Their job was to build towers, catapults and battering rams to smash down the walls. The biggest tower was called *Helepolis* or City-grabber. It was a wooden framework nine storeys high and armoured with metal sheets. It weighed 100 tons and ran on dozens of wheels; it took 3400 men to push it. The plan was to inch it up hard against the city wall; then, while archers and fire-throwers on the top storeys held the defenders at bay, men on the bottom storeys would dig their way through the wall below.

Unfortunately for Demetrius, his City-grabber took so long to build that the Rhodians had plenty

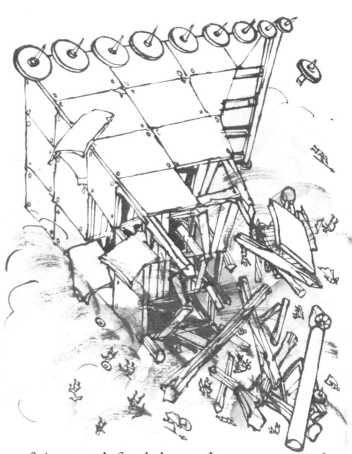

of time to defend themselves against it. They dug a tunnel under the city walls and across the plain towards Demetrius' men. It lay a metre or so (about three feet) below the surface, and no one could see it from above. When Demetrius' men trundled the City-grabber towards the walls, the tunnel roof fell in, the City-grabber fell on its side and its soldiers spilled out like beans from a split bag.

After this disaster, Demetrius

called off the siege, gathered his fleet, soldiers and engineers and sailed away. He left the City-grabber and his other siege engines where they lay, and as soon as he was gone the Rhodians decided to use the materials to make a thanksgiving to Helios for protecting them, to build him the biggest statue ever seen. They stripped off the metal armour-plating and melted it down; they sold the timber scaffolding and used the money to buy marble and stone and to pay a team of statue-builders led by the architect Chares.

Chares designed the statue to look like all the other Helios-statues on the island, large or small. It would show the god as a handsome prince. In his left hand he would hold a cloak (the cloak of darkness which the sun's light sweeps from the sky each morning). His right hand would be raised to his eyes (not to shade them from dazzle, but to direct their light-beams out across the world). A crown of spiky golden rays would surround his head. The only difference between this statue and all the others would

be its size: Chares planned to make it even bigger than the City-grabber had been, the first and most impressive sight visitors would see as they sailed towards the island.

Chares' men set up a marble platform for the statue to stand on. On it Chares mounted the statue's huge bronze feet. They were hollow, and each was so large that a dozen people could have crept inside and slept as comfortably as in a bed. After that, the workmen

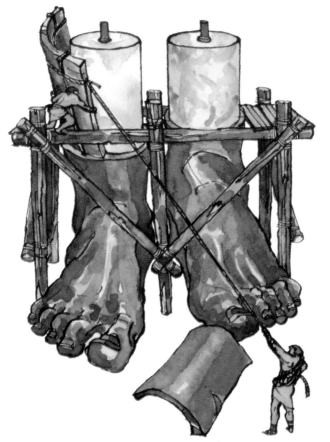

built the statue from the legs up, piece by piece. They shaped each new limb or joint in the workshop, carried it to the building-site and bolted it in place. Inside each metal leg was a marble pillar 1.5 metres (5 feet) in diameter, to lower the statue's centre of gravity and prevent it from toppling over. As soon as each hollow section was securely in place, the workmen filled it with a mixture of rubble and stones.

The statue was eighteen times human-size. It took twelve years to build, and when it was finished Chares' workmen polished its bronze skin till it glowed like the sun itself.

For the next fifty-six years the sun-statue stood in the heart of the city, looking out across the harbour. Then, in 224 BC, an earthquake rocked the island, snapped the statue off at the knees and sent it toppling across a whole city block. Instead of clearing it away or re-erecting it, the superstitious Rhodians left it lying, and it stayed in the same place for no less than another 900 years. It

26

Although the actual Colossus, converted into bronze coins, vanished entirely in the bazaars and markets of the Middle East, its fame lived on, and nearly twenty-two centuries after it was built it was reborn in a most unexpected way and in a place whose existence no ancient Rhodian would have known about. To celebrate the first centenary of the American Revolution of AD 1776, the French government gave the people of the USA a statue of Liberty, showing the goddess crowned with light-beams, dressed in flowing robes and holding the torch of freedom in one gigantic hand. The Statue of Liberty is 46 metres (152 feet) high, is made of hollow bronze, and stands at the entrance to New York harbour, welcoming visitors to the USA just as the giant Helios-statue once welcomed travellers to Rhodes.

THE GIANT OF RHODES

Date: c. 292–280 BC
Height: base c. 3 metres (10 feet);
  statue *c. 32 metres (105 feet)*
Weight: c. 20,320 kg (20 tons) of metal;
  c. 457,000 kg (c. 450 tons) of marble;
  unknown weight or rubble and concrete

lay like a fallen giant, and people visited Rhodes just to gape at its ruins. No one – not even the Romans, who called it *Colossus*, 'The Huge One', the origin of our word 'colossal' – thought of pillaging its valuable metal, until in

AD 654 a Syrian prince called Muswiyah captured Rhodes. He was fighting a war, and needed cash. He stripped the metal from the Colossus, dumped the rubble in the harbour, and shipped the bronze to the mainland.

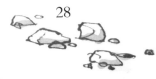

THE LIGHTHOUSE AT ALEXANDRIA

Whenever Alexander the Great added a new part of the world to his empire, he built a city there. (Many were called Alexandria after him.) There were two reasons. The new town would be a fortress, easy to defend and a stronghold for soldiers, and it would also be a showplace, advertising the glories of Greek civilisation to everyone in the area.

In 331 BC Alexander captured Egypt. His army marched there overland, across the Sinai desert. But he planned to leave in triumph, by ship, from one of the many mouths of the river Nile. (The Nile had so many mouths, all opening into the Mediterranean, that the Greeks called the area 'Delta' after the shape of their letter △.)

Every one of the Delta channels was shallow, clogged by silt and filled with treacherous rocks and currents. Since none of them was deep enough for a war-fleet, Alexander decided to build a new city, with a deep-water harbour ideal for both war-galleys and trading-ships. The site he chose was a narrow strip of land between Lake Mareotis and the sea, near one of the widest of all the river-mouths. The shoreline was long and low, and lay between two jutting-out claws of land; in front of it about 1200 metres (¾ mile) out to sea, was a large island called Pharos; the space between was sheltered and secure, ideal for a harbour.

Once, there had been nothing on the site but a small fishing-village. Alexander's workmen transformed it into a city. They built straight streets (in a grid-pattern like the one at Rhodes or Halicarnassus, easy to defend). They dug a canal between Lake Mareotis and the sea, and built shipyards, anchorages, docks and warehouses. Above all, they deepened the harbour, and used the dredged-up stones and mud to make a breakwater all the way from the city to Pharos island. It divided the harbour in two: one side for war-galleys, the other for merchant-ships.

The new city, Alexandria, remained a quiet seaport for twenty years. Then, after Alexander's death, his general Ptolemy took control of Egypt, made himself king, and chose Alexandria as his

29

royal capital. He and his son (who later became Ptolemy II) adorned it with temples, palaces, parks and race-courses, and turned it into one of the most dazzling cities in the ancient world.

Although Alexandria's twin harbours were deep and safe, sailors found it difficult to navigate their way into them. The entrances were narrow, and underwater currents funnelled through the rocks like rapids on a river. In 299 BC, therefore, Ptolemy II decided to build two beacons on Pharos island, to guide navigators safely through. On the western tip of the island he ordered a temple of Poseidon, god of the sea; on the eastern tip he ordered a fire-tower (or, as we would nowadays call it, a lighthouse).

The lighthouse was designed by a Greek architect called Sostratos. No one had ever made a lighthouse before, and his own experience had been in building city walls with massive gates and high, defensive towers. For this reason, he designed the *Pharos* (as the lighthouse was called, after the

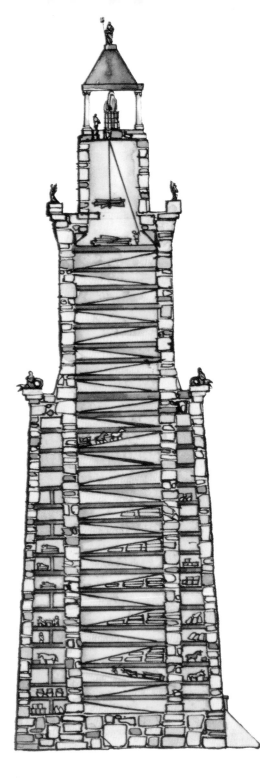

island it stood on) exactly like three towers, one on top of another. The base was a platform of massive stone blocks, two storeys high and strong enough to withstand the fiercest storm. On top of it was the first tower, a twenty-storey rectangular building filled with rooms like a modern apartment-building or block of flats, and big enough to house the lighthouse staff, a company of soldiers (in case the lighthouse was attacked), and the stable-hands who looked after the animals. On its flat roof was the second tower, hexagon-shaped and ten storeys high. This had no rooms, but contained a spiral pathway leading up to the final tower. (It was a pathway, not stairs, so that animals could easily be led up and down, carrying fuel for the fire.) The third tower was cylindrical (the shape of a modern lighthouse) and seven storeys high. At its top were the fire and mirrors that provided the light, and on its roof was a statue of the god Poseidon, towering forty storeys above the ground and gazing out across his sea-kingdom.

melted the Pharos' huge mirrors down for coins, took down Poseidon's statue and turned the topmost tower into a minaret, from whose balcony the *muezzin* called Muslim worshippers to morning, noon and evening prayer. In AD 1385 an earthquake toppled the two upper towers, and the Alexandrians converted the bottom one into a military fort designed to warn visitors away from the harbour rather than (as the lighthouse had) to welcome them. It has been built and rebuilt many times since, and a modern fort still marks the place where the lighthouse used to stand.

The lighthouse took nineteen years to build, and was lit for the first time in 280 BC. Its fuel was pine-branches, ferried to the island on barges and carried up the tower by pack-mules and (for the final stage) by a system of ropes and pulleys. Behind the fire, facing out to sea, was a set of curved bronze sheets the size of ships' sails. They were polished as smooth as mirror-glass, and reflected the light of the fire 48 kilometres (30 miles) out to sea. The lighthouse was in constant use for fourteen centuries. (In that time, it would have consumed the wood of several pine forests, over a million trees.) But by the twelfth century AD, when the Arabs ruled Alexandria, the harbour had become so clogged with silt that no ships could manoeuvre in or out. There was no more need of a lighthouse, and Alexandria's rulers

THE LIGHTHOUSE AT ALEXANDRIA

Date: c. 299–280 BC

Height: base *c.* 6 metres (20 feet);
  first tower *c.* 61 metres (200 feet);
  second tower *c.* 30 metres (100 feet));
  third tower *c.* 21 metres (70 feet);
  statue *c.* 6 metres (20 feet);
  total height *c.* 124 metres (410 feet).

Area: base *c.* 107 × 107 metres (350 × 350 feet); first tower a rectangle *c.* 30 × 30 metres (100 × 100 feet); second tower a hexagon *c.* 17 metres (55 feet) across, total perimeter *c.* 98 metres (220 feet), area *c.* 183 square metres (1965 square feet); third tower a cylinder *c.* 9 metres (30 feet) across, area 66 square metres (707 square feet).